I'M LUCKY - I BELIEVE...

Jack Bosomworth

with Tony Eaton

This edition edited by Philip Swan

Dedication

This book is dedicated to Frank, our mid-upper gunner, whose alertness saved us on that fateful Leipzig raid of the 19th/20th February, 1944. Sadly he went missing with his third crew later in the war.

Contents

	Introduction	1
Chapter 1	Early Days	4
Chapter 2	Service Life	8
Chapter 3	57 Squadron, Bomber Command	18
Chapter 4	O.T.U. Instructor	48
Chapter 5	Civvie Street	52

Introduction

No doubt some people will wonder why I have written this narrative. Well in the first place I was asked if I would do so. After due consideration I thought, 'what the hell, why not, it should be interesting! So with a lot of encouragement and help it came into being, involving much memory searching and nostalgia. Another reason was, it might help my family to see what their father or grandfather was really like under that blustery exterior and also the way he thought and reacted under times of stress. Maybe it could help them in the future.

With regards to my beliefs. I have tried not to preach, that is the last thing I would want to do! Most of what I have said evolved during my service with the Royal Air Force to give me a method of dealing with life (sometimes precarious) as it was then. It gave me peace of mind then, and I would not change it. I have been asked several times over the years about guilt. Have I not felt guilty about dropping bombs and being responsible for an unknown number of deaths? My answer is, No! There is no glorification in war, but when you get a man as evil as Hitler to contend with, appropriate action has to be taken. We were trained to do a job and carry out orders and that was that. In any case it was either 'them or us'.

Others were not quite so lucky and I lost some very good mates. Nevertheless, I do not believe in being bitter about it and do not bear any animosity towards the Germans. In fact I always say that next to us British, they are better than most. I have also been asked about fear. Yes, many times I was scared, very scared. But my biggest fear was that I would show it in front of my mates. I think that most people who have been in action would agree with me on that, whatever service they were in. Concerning Lady Luck - she has certainly been kind to me, or was it my 'Minder' doing an excellent job?

I consider myself to have been very lucky on three main counts. Firstly, that I chose and was accepted to fly in the RAF. I always consider my service to have been what I call my 'university of life'. Secondly, that I chose the pilot I did. Johnny Ludford could really handle a Lanc and on top of that he had an easy going authority when it came to handling men - all the crew worshipped him. Lastly, that I chose the right girl to be my wife. At the time of writing we have been together for fifty-four years. We have had our ups and downs as you might expect, both being ex-RAF types, but we have both landed together in the end - cross-wind or not.

What more can one want?

Jack Bosomworth, 1998

Chapter One

Early Days

The tiny hamlet of Kepwick where I was born on the 23rd of January 1922 is one of many hamlets and villages nestling at the foot of the Hambleton Hills in North Yorkshire. My parents were Tom and Ethel and I had a sister Joyce. Although I was born at Kepwick the family moved to Nether Silton where my father was a chauffeur to Mr Talbot, the estate agent for the Guthe shipping family, in the village of Kepwick. The car he drove as a chauffeur was a Model 'T 'Ford, then later elevating to a Bull Nosed Morris. One of the duties my father had to perform for Mr. Talbot was an annual run to Nairn in Scotland for long fishing trips, and he had some interesting tales to tell about those trips. Later the Talbot family left and a Captain Stephens took over the running of the estate. My mother, apart from looking after my sister and me, worked in service as a house maid in Kepwick Hall. Dad was also the unofficial village barber as there wasn't one in those times and a round trip to Northallerton was a long awkward journey. The men who needed a haircut would come along to our house where my father would snip away. Being a smoker he charged the local workers a packet of ten Woodbines per haircut, but if he cut the hair of anyone who was considered to be well off, he charged them a packet of ten Players. Sometimes when the light was failing during the haircutting sessions and there being no electricity to the house, I was given the job of holding a candle to illuminate the room, following my father around as he cut each side of the head. Once when Dad wasn't available, four young men arrived at the house needing a haircut prior to going to a dance. I volunteered to cut their hair and made a reasonable job of it I'm proud to say, and collected the Woodbines!

I attended the Church of England school in Nether Silton and stayed there until I was fourteen years old, and the Church of England played a large part in my upbringing. Although the family was C of E my mother would take both me and my sister Joyce to the church and chapel in the village on alternate Sundays, so by the time I had reached my teens I had a fair grounding on the church, and religion in general. In any case there was very little else to do on those quiet village Sundays. On reaching the age of eleven I sat and passed the Eleven Plus school exam, but in those days an interview for Northallerton Grammar School was a requirement before a pupil could be accepted. I duly went for the interview which consisted of simple mathematical sums and general knowledge questions. However, the real purpose of the interview was to enquire and evaluate the status of my parents. I really think that because my father was a chauffeur and my mother in service I was considered unsuitable material for the Grammar School. This decision was a huge disappointment for me and left me a little upset and angry with perhaps a bit of a chip on my shoulder. However, being turned down for the Grammar School brought out in me a determination to succeed in everything that I tried.

I hid my disappointment and carried on my schooling at Nether Silton School. At the age of fourteen years and six months I finally left and took on a job as a labourer with Potter's Builders of Thimbleby, helping to build part of Over Silton Hall. However this work lasted only six months when I applied for a job at Barker's Store in Northallerton. I was accepted and offered the wage of 8/6 per week plus commission. In those days getting to and from work from those outlying villages often meant either walking or cycling. Nether Silton is some eight miles from Northallerton so I had to cycle to work. My first ever bicycle was a ladies sit-up-and-beg model and it was hard work pedalling those eight miles, but nothing was ever thought of it as that was the way most people travelled. At Barkers I was employed in the Lino and floor covering department, but later I moved to the menswear department where I was trained in measuring men for their suits. The measuring dept was a job that I really took to and found a lot of pleasure in the work. After I had been at Barkers a few months I bought myself a brand new bike, a Rudge/Whitworth which cost me 2/6 a week on the never-never, and costing £5 in all.

Like a lot of country boys I was interested in sport, the usual football and cricket. My first love was cricket and by the time I had left school I was playing regularly for Nether Silton. I suppose I might have been called an all rounder which sounds rather grand, but I did bat and bowl for the team, with bowling being my preference at what might be described as medium pace. During my time working at Barkers I would often go to a sweet shop close by and it was there that I met the girl who was to become my future wife. Her name was Dorothy Eyles and she worked as a clerical assistant for Boston's Bakery and lived at Leeming Bar. We got into conversation with one another in the sweet shop and became very friendly which eventually led to me plucking up the courage to ask her out. Quite a courageous thing for a shy country boy.

By September 1939 the country was once again at war with Germany. Although I was only seventeen and half years old and too young to join up, my thoughts were already turning to the probability of call-up for military service. But in the meantime I continued working at Barkers Store. Shortly after the Battle of Britain had ended, I was asked to measure an RAF officer for a new uniform. That officer was Flying Officer Bennions, DFC, who lived at Catterick. He was a Spitfire pilot who had flown with 41 Squadron and had lost an eye fighting in the Battle of Britain but had recovered enough to still serve. Although I did not know the circumstances of his injuries, and they must have been horrific, simply speaking to him and seeing him all resplendent in his uniform complete with his wings and medal ribbon made me decide to join the RAF at the earliest possible moment. I was determined to volunteer when I was old enough as I just did not fancy being called up for the army and being dressed in khaki. I also had visions of mud and trench warfare as I had read and heard about in the Great War. For me it was to be the RAF and as a flyer. In the summer of 1941 I eventually volunteered for the RAF just prior to registering for call up. I was given the usual entrance exam and a medical. I passed with ease the written exam, but to my dismay I failed the medical due to a slightly perforated right ear drum. The Medical Officer said I was fit enough for ground crew duties but not aircrew. As a volunteer I insisted that I wanted to fly and refused to accept a ground crew post. The reply to that was try again in three months time. I was so determined to fly that I said I would come back then. In the meantime I was given treatment for my damaged ear at Harrogate Hospital.

So some three months later I went before the medical board once again, and by chance and guessing correctly what the doctor said in the hearing test I passed and was accepted as being fit for aircrew. I was selected for training as a wireless operator/air gunner. As long as it was aircrew I did not mind. That was the first hurdle which gave me the confidence and spirit to try my utmost for what lay ahead. My resolve to succeed which all began with my rejection for the Grammar School was all the more fierce. I returned home to Nether Silton and waited for the arrival of the papers telling me I was to join the RAF. The papers duly arrived informing me that I was to report to RAF Station Padgate near Warrington in Lancashire. I was now in the Royal Air Force. What lay ahead, I wondered. Life was never to be the same!

Chapter Two

Service Life

On October 7th 1941 I arrived at RAF Padgate Recruit Training Centre near Warrington in Lancashire. Arriving with me were hundreds of other raw young men with the same bewildered look on their faces as me. Coming straight from a small country village into an RAF camp seething with all manner of people from all walks of life with a host of corporals and sergeants shouting and bawling orders was quite a shock. At Padgate I was given my rank and number. From that time I was to be known as . . . . 1479620 Aircraftman 2nd Class. Bosomworth. J.T.

We were issued with the usual plethora of kit deemed necessary for raw RAF recruits. It was here that I was introduced to what the 'Sprog' airmen indelicately called 'Bullshit', most of which seemed to be of the baffling variety. That is, the seemingly endless and pointless cleaning and polishing of brasses, badges and boots. However, all this didn't last long. Some four days later a whole host of us were packed off to Blackpool just a few miles from Padgate where we were all billeted in civilian digs. There were twenty one of us somehow fitted into No. 35 Dixon Road, a huge house run by a Mrs. Wallwork. She treated us all very well considering the sheer hard work involved looking after so many noisy, and at times, awkward young men. At Blackpool I was taught how to march, salute and generally act like an airman. One of the sergeant Drill Instructors or DI's as we called them, was Jack London the pre-war boxer and father of the future heavyweight boxer Brian London; Peter Kane, a pre-war boxer of some fame was another. Another drill instructor there was Max Wall the comedian and although he was in charge of another squad the news filtered through that he treated the recruits like dirt. Despite being so disliked, this didn't stop him from obtaining tickets for his weekly radio show at the Opera House for some of his recruits. Another hazard recruits had to face was a series of inoculations. The result of these 'Jabs' was a whole group of sprog airmen walking around with aching stiff arms with a look of misery on their faces. After one particular nasty injection I was walking along the street in Blackpool with a couple of pals, all with our right arms held out in discomfort, when we were approached by a cockney airman. He asked, "ave you just had a jab?" when we told him we had he said, "Go to the chemist along the road there and 'e will sell you a special draft for a couple of bob which will get rid of the aches and pains". We thought it was worth a try and paid our 2/- for a dose and it wasn't long before we were pain free. I have often wondered if that cockney lad was in the pay of the chemist to drum up business. Another amusing incident when we were being given our course of jabs was when one lad, Bob Taylor, who was quite short received a double dose. The chap in front of Bob was 6'4" and Bob was 5'4" and the jabs were given in rapid succession along a queue of airmen standing with arms on their hips. There were no such refinements as stopping to change the needle and the tall guy fainted and fell. Before Bob could get out of the way after his first jab into his bent arm held out in a 'Pansy' pose, he had the needle stuck into his arm again! As a result he received a double dose, that is 150% instead of 75%. To put it mildly, he was rather poorly.

It was at Blackpool where I was given my first course on becoming a wireless operator/air Gunner, but the emphasis was on the wireless operating side. The gunnery training was to come later. The course was a basic introduction to wireless operating dwelling chiefly on learning Morse Code. The required rate of transmitting and receiving Morse Code was eighteen words per minute. Anything less and you failed. I struggled at first but eventually passed after a re-sit exam at ten words per minute. During my training at Blackpool our billet was next door to another house containing a group of female civil servants who were employed doing clerical work for the RAF. Each of us fancied our chances with these girls, so we devised a method of communicating with them by using Morse Code and tapping messages on the wall, after passing them a copy of the Morse Code. We used a fork for the 'dots' and a small brush for the dashes. Through these series of coded messages, we organised a date with four girls who I might add were very willing. With me being rather naive and shy, and last out of the door, I ended up with the one nobody would have chosen if given the choice! As quick as I could I rushed her into the darkness of the nearest cinema. All of this was harmless fun especially for me. I was nineteen years old and it was more to prove we could make a date with the girls by the methods we used than anything else. She seemed to be a respectable girl in any case. Dorothy and I were writing to each other on a regular basis, and it was about this time she told me that she was going to volunteer for the WAAF. So both of us would be dressed in RAF blue.

In January 1942 I was posted from Blackpool to No 4 Radio School at RAF Yatesbury in Wiltshire. It was at Yatesbury where I hoped I was at last going to fly with the RAF. My interest increased as the chance of flying came ever nearer. But I was in for a shock. I developed phlebitis in both my inner thighs and as a result of this illness I was taken off the course and packed off to hospital for a couple of weeks. After leaving hospital I was given fourteen days sick leave, returning in time to join another squad and completed the course. In the final exam I got enough marks to be promoted to Aircraftsman 1st Class (AC1). My education at Silton 'High School' (the one on the hill?) had not included electrics and kindred matters so I found it hard work keeping up with grammar school types and higher. So the night before the final exam I sketched a small elementary electrical circuit on each finger nail, a long laborious job but one which paid off as three of the circuits on my nails were among the questions in the exam. With the exam well and truly over I was able to wash my hands once again.

From Yatesbury I was posted to RAF Topcliffe which was about eight miles from where I lived. The reason I and many other airmen were moved was that there were far too many men being pushed though the training schools and the system simply could not cope. I had a marvellous time at Topcliffe, travelling home most week ends on my

Certificates of Qualification.
(to be filled in as appropriate)

1. This is to certify that J.T. Bosomworth 1479620
   has qualified as W/OP (AIR-CREW)
   with effect from 19 APR 1943 Sgd. W Clark F/L.
   Date 19 APR 1943 Unit NO. 4 R.S.

2. This is to certify that ....
   has qualified as ....
   with effect from ....
   Date ....

3. This ....
   has ....
   with ....
   Date ....

4. This is to certify that ....
   has qualified as ....
   with effect from .... Sgd. ....
   Date .... Unit ....

NIGHT VISION	27
	32
DATE	12.2.43

bike and enjoying walking around in my uniform. After I had been at Topcliffe for a couple of months I was being asked by the local people such things as, 'When are you going back?' and, 'When does your leave finish?' So when I was finally called in September 1942 to resume my training at RAF Madley near Hereford I was glad to be away. Being fully fit and clear of the phlebitis, I was re-coursed and got back to the flying which I had so much been looking forward to. The aircraft in which we were going to fly and learn our trade was the De Haviland Rapide, known as the Dominie to the RAF, and the Percival Proctor. The Dominie was a graceful twin engined bi-plane which had been used to carry passengers and freight in the 1930s and was ideal for training. After weeks of ground training I had my first ever flight in a Dominie, as a trainee wireless operator on the 16th of February 1943, which was piloted by Flying Officer Bradshaw. The flight lasted one hour and thirty-five minutes, my first of many hours learning the intricacies of operating the standard wireless equipment of the RAF. The early training consisted of Direction Finding (DF) tuning with 'Q' code and frequency changing and calibration. All of the flying was done in daylight and on the Dominie aircraft, except for two flights in a Proctor totalling one hour and fifty-five minutes. The training all through was fairly intense and by the end of the course on the 4th of April 1943 I had logged twenty-four hours and twenty-five minutes flying time. I successfully completed my course and the next stage of training came a step nearer. I had my Log Book stamped confirming that I was now qualified as a wireless operator.

At that time all wireless operators had a dual role and were also required to be proficient as air gunners. From Madley I was then posted to RAF Manby in Lincolnshire to do my training as an air gunner. This course was very short. lasting a mere two weeks and consisted of ground training which required firing the guns from a fixed turret on the ground at moving targets. I was destined to fly with Bomber Command and so the ground gunnery course was considered sufficient, as my primary role would be as a wireless operator. If I had been designated to be posted to other commands I would then have had to complete the full flying gunners course. I completed my gunnery training with reasonable results and was then posted to RAF Bobbington in the Midlands, now known as Halfpenny Green. Completing the course was a proud moment for me, especially when on the 19th April I was awarded the coveted 'S' for Signaller flying badge and my stripes. From that moment I was officially known as . . . .

1479620 Sergeant Bosomworth. J.T.

I arrived at Bobbington at the beginning of June by which time I had cultivated a moustache and which was to be a permanent fixture of my features, and I'm glad to say met with Dorothy's approval. Within a few days of arriving I was airborne once again, learning the more advanced aspects of wireless operating relevant to operational flying. The aircraft we used at this stage of our training was the Avro Anson, a slow twin engined aircraft which had entered the war with Coastal Command but had since been relegated to flying training. The 'Annie' as it was called was reliable but uncomfortable and one of the chores delegated to trainee air crew in the Annie was the laborious task of winding up and winding down the undercarriage. No such luxury as a hydraulic system in the old Annie. Our training consisted of Cross Country QDM, QTE fixes and Loops. Also for the first time I flew at night which was quite an experience and a foretaste of what was to come. After completing this phase of my training the whole course was given fourteen days very welcome leave.

It wasn't long before I received my next move and this was to RAF Wymeswold, the home of No. 28 Operational Training Unit. (O.T.U.) It was at O.T.U. that the nitty gritty of flying training really began. First we were 'crewed up' - an interesting experience! Twenty of each crew positions, pilot, navigator, bomb aimer, wireless operator and rear gunner, were paraded together in a large hangar. (The flight engineer and mid/upper gunners were to be added later as the aircraft we were training on was the five man Wellington) We were told to sort ourselves out into twenty complete crews. It seemed rather an odd way of going about it but apparently it worked. After gazing about for ten minutes I caught the eye of a short fair haired pilot sitting casually on the edge of a table smoking a cigarette. He looked quiet and cool and something seemed to say 'He's the one for you Buzz', (Buzz was the nickname I had acquired which was a shortened version of my surname). The pilot looked back at me with his pale blue eyes as I walked across and introduced myself, at the same time asking if he had got himself a wireless operator. He said,

'No I haven't'. I said, 'You have now'. It was one of the best decisions I ever made and I learned later to worship the guy. We wandered around the hangar amongst the milling aircrew and eventually persuaded three other 'Bods' to join us. We eventually finished with a crew as follows:

Pilot	Sgt. Johnny Ludford from Ealing London.
Navigator	P/O. Ron Watson from Glasgow.
Bomb Aimer	Sgt. John Woodbridge from Suffolk.
Rear Gunner	F/Sgt. Red Saigion from Saskatchewan Canada.
Wireless Operator	Sgt. Jack Bosomworth

We were later to be joined by two other crew members at the Conversion Unit. One was, mid-upper gunner Sgt. Des Green of

The Crew

Norfolk, who was later replaced by Frank Fox of London due to illness. Sadly Des Green was lost after he returned to operations flying with another crew. Frank Fox wore a wound stripe on his sleeve as a result of being shot up while flying with another crew. The other crew member was flight engineer Sgt. Maurice Stoneman, just eighteen years old and a fitness fanatic. So there we were seven men who were going to war and who would very soon have to mould together as a team!

Lancaster D - Dog

On the 13th July I took my first flight in a bomber. The bomber was the Vickers Wellington, a twin engined aircraft which, along with the Hampden and the Whitley, had spearheaded Bomber Command's offensive against Germany in the early years of the war. By 1943 the Wellington was being withdrawn from the main bomber force as the newer and larger trio of four engined heavy bombers, the Stirling, Halifax and Lancaster, came into service. The first three weeks of our training at 28 O.T.U was all day flying which allowed us to become familiar with the aircraft and it's equipment. The training at the O.T.U. consisted of practice bombing, navigation cross-country flights, air-to-air and air-to-sea firing for the gunners, together with dinghy drill, an extremely important part of our training in case we were forced to ditch in the sea. I am pleased to say that we held the record for evacuating five crew members from an aircraft. We were timed at 16.5 seconds. After we had completed eighteen hours of day flying we began our night flying training. The course was very intensive and the old training aircraft had hardly time to get cold before they were in the air with another crew. Several came to grief and I recall on one day we had flown two to three hours on O-Oboe and landed safely. After a couple of hours turn round it was taken up by another 'Sprog' crew and immediately crashed killing all occupants. To crown our shock we were called up to be the burial party. Such events made one think, but it didn't do to dwell! I felt I was beginning to use up my spare luck. On the 21st of August we completed our training at Wymeswold and were sent home on leave to await our next move.

Early September I arrived at No. 1654 Conversion Unit Wigsley. The aircraft used for training at Wigsley was the spectacular Lancaster, so this told us we would be going onto a Lancaster squadron on completion of our Conversion training. The training at Wigsley was similar to the training at Wymeswold but this time with a crew of seven, as we had acquired our flight engineer and mid-upper gunner. That crew was the seven men with whom I would go on operational flying when we were posted to a bomber squadron and that day was drawing ever nearer. It was at Wigsley that we experienced our one and only crash or crash landing. We had been detailed for a training flight where we carried a full dummy bomb load, so the aircraft had the all-up weight as if we were on operations. The idea was for us to take off and fly on a certain heading for several hours and then return to base. On the return leg the Skipper found that we had problems with the brakes of the aircraft. As a precaution he ordered all the crew to take up 'crash stations'. The crash stations were specially selected places in the aircraft where crew members were considered to be the most safe in the event of an expected crash. The Skipper brought the Lanc straight in and he was right, the brakes were faulty. The bomber kept on going and we crashed through the boundary fence and landed in the next field. Fortunately none of the crew received any injuries. Luck was with us.

There was one special manoeuvre which we practised with the Lanc at the Con Unit which was of vital importance to every bomber crew's survival when on operations. That manoeuvre was know as the 'cork-screw'. The cork-screw was a series of manoeuvres carried out by the pilot with instructions given usually by the two gunners. The basics of the manoeuvre were that the gunner would tell the Skipper to cork-screw to port if the attack was coming from port and starboard if coming from that direction. The principle being that the bomber would turn and dive into the attack, the oncoming enemy fighter would then over shoot and pass the bomber. If anticipated early and action taken directly it was sometimes enough to lose the fighter as the separation distance increased with both aircraft flying in different directions. This manoeuvre was always practiced on fighter affiliation exercises.

On the 16th of October as a crew we had our last flight with 1654 Conversion Unit Wigsley. All the training and instruction we had done together was now to be put to the test as we awaited a posting to a squadron, but which one?

Chapter Three

57 Squadron, Bomber Command

The home of 57 Squadron was at Royal Air Force East Kirkby, near Boston, in Lincolnshire just recently opened, eventually becoming the home of 630 Squadron which started operational life as a flight of 57 Squadron. I arrived with the rest of my crew at East Kirkby in late October and we were soon airborne in a Lancaster, training with 'A' Flight of the squadron. The training was more intense and included a lot of high level bombing and what were known as 'Bullseye' exercises. Bullseye was a name given to an exercise where a bomber would practice a bombing run on a town or city in the UK in order to both test the city warning systems and the crew of the bomber. By the time we had all gathered at East Kirkby John Ludford had received his commission and was now a pilot officer.

It was at this time that Dorothy and I became what you might say unofficially engaged. There was no formal announcement to parents or a formal proposal by me, it was simply a joint decision. It happened one day when we were at Northallerton railway station as I was returning from leave. We more or less said we would get married, and now that I was a sergeant and Dorothy a corporal we thought the time had come for us to make the decision. The decision, however, was to prove more difficult than we both realised. The wing commander would not grant special leave until we had completed at least one operational sortie. The Skipper had also put in for compassionate leave to see his brother who had just returned from South Africa. So both of us just had to be patient.

One of our first tasks was to go to RAF Syerston in Nottinghamshire to collect a brand new Lanc, D-Dog. This was our Lanc in which we would go on operations, and in which we would fight our war. After fourteen days of training with D-Dog, the squadron commander considered us competent enough to be put on operations. Our last training trip was a daylight NFT exercise on the 18th of November 1943, and so now the training was over it was our turn to go to war. That very night we were on Ops.

I should like to give a resume of the duties of a wireless operator within Bomber Command. Firstly, when an Op was 'on' all w/ops would attend a special brief to be given the call signs, a stop watch and the 'colour of the day'. The colour of the day was the colour of the pyrotechnic flares that were to be dropped by the Pathfinders to indicate the target. This information was extremely secret, and if the Germans were to discover the colour of the day they could and would imitate them and drop the same coloured flares into the open countryside, thus misdirecting the bomber stream. So secret was that information given to the w/ops, that it was written on a piece of rice paper, which could be eaten if need be. En-route the w/op was to listen out to Group HQ every half hour for instructions and messages and to give the wind speeds and directions. This kept the bomber stream on course. The Morse Code callsign for 5 Group was 9SY . I can hear it yet coming over loud and clear through my earphones.

During the period of my tour a device called 'Fishpond' was tried out. Fishpond was an anti-fighter device incorporated into the H2S system (H2S was a navigation and target identification radar). It had a scope with distance rings on it where I would watch for anything out of the ordinary in aircraft movement. If a blip came in from a different angle and at speed toward the bombers then it was possibly a night fighter, and I would advise the Skipper accordingly. One had to be certain it was a German as sometimes we had Mosquitoes in the bomber stream. I would keep watch on the Fishpond on the run-into the target, but over the target I would man the astro dome on the top of the fuselage. I was an extra pair of eyes as a look out for night fighters. This was really forbidden as one w/op had had his head shot off during an attack, but our Skipper preferred another look out, and after all, he was my boss.

The battle orders on the 18th of November 1943 listed the names of our crew. This was it! All the training, all the hard work of the previous months, was now to be put to the test. Team work was to be the key. Each crew had to work as a team to ensure a successful operational sortie and to ensure the crews safety. We were called to the briefing room to learn what the target was to be, and be given the met report and the disposition of the German defences etc.

We walked into the briefing room where our eyes were drawn to the large blackboard on the far wall. On that wall there hung a huge map of Europe. A length of red cotton stretched from East Kirkby on a 'dog-leg' route across Europe to Berlin! Our very first Op was to be the Big City of Berlin. All crews hoped for what might be considered an 'easy' Op for the first one, but for us there was no such luck. I was to learn, as did all bomber crews, that there was no such thing as an 'easy' Op. What was easy for some turned out to be a nightmare trip for others and vice versa. However there was no mistaking the severity of our very first Op with 57 Squadron. We didn't know it at the time, but this raid on Berlin was the opening phase of what was to be called the Battle of Berlin, a concentrated series of attacks on the German capital.

When the CO came into the room we all stood to attention and then were requested to be seated. A string of officers then came to the stage and gave their information. The met officer, the intelligence officer, the gunnery and navigation leaders all gave their assessment of what was to be expected and any foreseen problems. When the brief was over we all traipsed out of the room and went into the changing room and donned our flying kit. The poor old rear gunner had to struggle into layer after layer of kit all designed to keep out the intense cold in his lonely part of the aircraft. For my part I was rather fortunate. The w/op's 'office' was one of the warmest places in the whole aircraft so I was not issued with such cumbersome clothing. After putting on our flying clothing we waited for the time to climb aboard the crew bus which took us out to our Lanc. All aircrew were offered a service revolver for personal protection if ever they were shot down and lost in enemy territory. I declined the offer, thinking that when it came to it the Germans had bigger and more guns than I would have, so it would be no contest. That was not for me, I bought myself a sheath knife, but not for defence but for surviving in a strange country.

The crew bus arrived and we heaved ourselves aboard complete with all the paraphernalia carried by all crew members. We would board the aircraft with everybody turning right except the rear gunner who turned left after hauling in the ladder. Each one of us had a series of checks and tests to carry out on our own particular pieces equipment. After the checks we would then disembark and sit around waiting.

I would like to relate some of the checks and procedures carried out by the Skipper and the flight engineer. These two members of the crew were responsible for keeping the aircraft flying and maintaining the many systems on board. In short, to keep the nuts and bolts more or less together, in order to get us to the target and to get us back. The debt the rest of the crew owed to these two members cannot be overestimated. After the crew checked in on the intercom the Skipper and flight engineer would then begin the engine run up.

The job of the flight engineer started just as soon as he arrived at the dispersal to carry out the external checks. These included checking the wheels, tyres, the trolley acc. for starting, and that there were no external locks on the control surfaces. On reaching the cockpit he would assist the Skipper with his safety harness and then go through the start up procedure and switch on his panel to check fuel levels. A thumbs up to the ground crew operating the trolley acc. He would press the starter for the appropriate engine which in order of firing was - Port Outer - Port Inner - Starboard Outer - Starboard Inner. When all the engines were running and the temperatures and pressures were OK, a signal was made to the ground crew to remove the trolley acc. Then he would switch the Ground/Flight switch to Ground.

The Skipper would then signal the ground crew to remove the chocks and would then taxi the aircraft out of dispersal. Both would check the pressures and look at the runway controller's caravan. There was always a group of 'Bods' next to the caravan to see the bombers off. As soon as the green signal was given for us to take off, that was when the Skipper and flight engineer took over. Then a green 'Go' light from the controller. There was always strict radio silence. The f/e would switch on the Pitot Head heater on his panel. The Skipper would say to all the crew, "stand by for take off". He would then apply the brakes, open up to 0 on the boost, release the brakes and 65,000lbs of Lancaster would roll forward. The Skipper would then open the throttles, leading with the port to counter a tendency to swing to port. As soon as the tail wheel left the ground (a level floor at last), the f/e took control of the throttles. The Skipper would ask for 'full power' and the f/e would advance the throttles by pushing from the bottom of the levers so that in an emergency the Skipper could take control and the f/e's hands would not be in the way. A slight restriction at the 'gate', then through to the 'stops'. The friction nut would then be tightened to prevent the throttle retarding. A quick glance at his panel for no warning lights or wrong temps or pressures. With 3,000 rpm and 14lbs Boost he would then start calling out the speed in knots for the Skipper, 70 - 85 - 90 - 100 - 105, then the vibrating stops and there is just the roar of the four Merlins and we are over the boundary fence.

The skipper calls, "Brakes on - wheels up". The f/e repeats and raises the undercarriage. He then tells him that there are red lights which means the u/c is up, the lights go out, and the u/c is locked.

The Skipper then asks for five degrees of flap. The f/e would pull all the flaps in, we were then well and truly airborne. We would orbit and rendezvous with the rest of the squadron - the trip was on.

As I stated earlier our first Op was the opening phase of the Battle of Berlin. I would like to give a resumé of the Battle and reasons for it.

Berlin - The Main Battle

The Battle of Berlin began on the 18/19th of November 1943, and in the words of the C-in-C of Bomber Command, Air Marshal 'Butch' Harris, "Bomber Command will wreck Berlin from end to end". It was reasoned that hitting the German capital in a long sustained bombing campaign would hasten the war's end by convincing the German people of the futility of the war. This reasoning was also used for the whole of the Bomber Offensive, but hitting their capital was the crux of the campaign. For the crews of the 'Command', Berlin was the most daunting of targets. Other targets were as well defended as 'The Big City' as the crews called Berlin, especially the targets in the Ruhr Valley, but Berlin was the one that caused the most consternation. This phase of the bomber offensive was to last until the middle of February 1944. Although there was to be one more raid by the heavy formations in March, it was the Mosquito which was to take over the role as the Berlin Bomber. The Germans defended their capital with great courage, skill and tenacity, a tenacity that was to stretch the courage and endurance of the bomber crews to their uttermost limits. So, on 18th of November 1943, one of the most severe and bitter air battles of the Second World War was about to be joined .

I will give a brief summary of how the operation affected us as a crew and anything of note that happened during the trip. I will then follow it with the resumé of the actual raid as related by Martin Middlebrook and Chris Everitt in their magnificently researched book The Bomber Command War Diaries. I would also like to point out that what was a successful trip for us was not necessarily a successful trip from the point of view of Bomber Command.

For this raid and almost every other, we carried the standard Lancaster bomb load. This consisted of a 4,000lb bomb, 'The Cookie'; four General Purpose high explosive bombs; and, several containers of 4lb incendiaries. So this was it, my first operational sortie. I was going to war. I settled into my position and as we began the take-off run with those four Merlin engines bellowing; it was then my little bit of religious upbringing came to the fore. I closed my eyes, clasped my hands together and said a prayer to My God. I asked for deliverance and safety. I had a strange ambivalence toward religion and the church, I was no angel, but despite all this I still had a belief and this belief would, I hoped, carry me through the war and beyond. I had given quite some thought to this. In my own simple way I decided that no one being or power could possibly be responsible for everything or everyone. It wasn't feasible. So I brought into being my own God - a type of minder or guide 'on the other side'. I gave him a name and he became my mentor with whom I could talk things over.

Not just for myself but for my friends and relatives. He has helped me all my life and I would not be without him. Everyone should have something to worship. Now you know mine!

Once airborne I settled down to my tasks which helped to take my mind off what lay ahead. The approach to the target was fairly quiet (for us) and then when we were over the target we went into the bombing run. We all heard John Woodbridge, the bomb aimer, say those longed for words 'Bombs Gone' and the Skipper put D-Dog in a diving turn and we headed for home. After calling 'Silksheen', the callsign given to East Kirkby flying control, we landed safely after a trip lasting eight hours and five minutes. As we touched down I offered a prayer of thanks. We climbed aboard the crew bus and went to the debrief, which was always obligatory after every Op. We gave our version of events to the Intelligence Officer, had some breakfast and went to our bunks and slumped into bed. We had come through our first operational sortie safely and carried out our duties efficiently. I pondered on the coming twenty-nine and so did the rest of my crew I am sure.

Berlin 18/19th November 1943.
There were 440 Lancasters and four Mosquitoes on this raid. The force was intercepted by a few fighters. Berlin was completely cloud covered and both marking and bombing were carried out 'blind'. Bomber Command could make no assessment of the results. The local Berlin report shows that bombs fell in most parts of the city but no main concentration could be detected, although southern districts were hit more than others. Four industrial premises were totally destroyed and twenty-eight damaged. Eleven explosive works and four chemical plants were among the figures. There were 169 houses destroyed and 476 seriously damaged. Casualties were - 113 people killed, fourteen missing and 391 injured. Twenty-seven of the killed were foreign workers or POWs. Nine Lancasters were lost, 2.0% of the force.

I had now completed that one Op the Wingco had said that we must do, so Dorothy and I began the process of getting married. It was a frantic effort acquiring all the necessary documents and permission, one of which was special dispensation and license by the Bishop of Ripon for us to be married. We were both given leave and on Wednesday the 24th of November 1943 we were married at Leeming village church. We caught the train from Northallerton and headed to Blackpool for a four day honeymoon. We had the pleasure of staying in the same digs in which I was billeted when I was doing my early training. I also had the pleasure of meeting some of the drill instructors from those days and even more pleasure at seeing that they were still corporals and I was a sergeant. I suppose this rather selfish reaction was part of my determination to succeed. All too soon the honeymoon was over and I had to get back to the war. We didn't make any arrangements to try and live together but decided to live our lives at our respective stations and meet on week ends and when we were on leave. So we set sail into married life in the middle of a war and with me directly involved in it. There must have been some faith somewhere in our makeup I am sure.

I got back to East Kirkby in time for our crew's second Op and once more it was the Big City - Berlin. Our crew were really being thrown in at the deep end, but there was nothing for it but grin and bear it. On the take-off run I said my prayer, the same prayer which I said on my first Op, that was to be repeated on each occasion that I took off on an operational sortie. En-route to the target the r/t intercom went u/s which meant we couldn't speak to one another. Through a series of signals the Skipper asked if we should press on and the answer was yes. I was rather proud of that vote as we were entitled to return to base with such a problem. That problem apart it was another straight run for us, but two aircraft from the squadron failed to return (FTR) Altogether forty bombers were lost that night. After a trip lasting seven hours and twenty-five minutes we landed safely back at base.

Berlin 2/3rd December 1943.
There were 458 aircraft on this raid, 425 Lancasters, Eighteen Mosquitoes and fifteen Halifaxes. There was no major diversions and the bombers took a direct route across the North Sea to Holland and then to Berlin. The Germans identified Berlin as the target nineteen minutes before Zero Hour and many fighters were waiting there. Incorrectly forecast winds scattered the bomber stream, particularly on the return trip and German fighters scored further victories here. Those inaccurate wind forecast caused great difficulties for the Pathfinders who were not able to establish their position properly.

The bombing photographs of the main force suggested the attack was scattered over a wide area of southern Berlin and the countryside. The Berlin report confirms this but adds that some damage was caused in industrial areas of eastern and western districts with two Siemen factories, a ball bearing factory, and several railway stations being badly hit. Damage elsewhere was light, only 136 buildings being destroyed. Thirty six people were killed and a further 105 missing. As the bomber offensive progressed the German reports became increasingly erratic. The final report for this raid is missing from the Berlin archives. Forty aircraft were lost, of these thirty-seven were Lancasters, two Halifaxes and one Mosquito, 8.7% of the force. 460 RAAF Squadron lost five of the twenty-five

Lancasters despatched including the aircraft in which two newspaper reporters were flying. These were Captain Grieg of the Daily Mail and Norman Stockton of the Sydney Sun. The body of Mr. Stockton lies buried in the Berlin cemetery.

After but a few hours sleep it was Ops once again. The target was Leipzig where we made a heading for Berlin before diverting to our real target. This ploy was often used to try and confuse the German controllers and fighters. This sometimes worked but occasionally the Germans correctly guessed the real target and assembled scores of fighters to meet the bomber stream on the way to and over the target. For us it was another quiet trip lasting seven hours and fifty minutes and thankfully all the squadron aircraft returned safely.

Leipzig 3/4th December 1943.
There were 527 aircraft on this raid. Of these 307 were Lancasters and 220 Halifaxes. Despite the loss of two pressmen the previous night the famous American broadcaster Ed Murrow flew on this raid with a 619 Squadron Lancaster crew. He returned safely. The main force took another direct route to Berlin before turning off to Leipzig. The German fighters got amongst the bomber stream and scored many successes before the turn to Leipzig was made. Most of the fighters then turned to Berlin when a Mosquito diversion force bombed there. There were few fighters over Leipzig and only three bombers were lost over the target area, two being shot down by flak. This was a relatively successful raid from the view point of bomber casualties. However, this was spoiled when many aircraft flew by mistake to Frankfurt's defended area, where more than half the aircraft lost on that night were shot down there.

The Pathfinders found and marked this distant target and the bombing was very effective and turned out to be the most successful raid on Leipzig of the war. A large area of housing and many industrial premises were severely damaged. One place which was hit by a large number of bombs was the former World Fair exhibition site whose spacious buildings had been converted to become war factories, the largest being the Junkers Aircraft Company. The British official history quotes the Leipzig city records as giving a figure of 1,182 people killed, but a local German report compiled a week after the raid gives different figure - 614 people killed and 464 injured. It is not known which report is correct. Twenty-four aircraft were lost, fifteen Halifaxes and nine Lancasters, 4.6% of the force.

After the Leipzig raid we were given seven days leave which was very welcome and gave Dorothy and I a chance to meet for more than a brief weekend. The leave came to an end far too quickly and on the

13th of December it was back to East Kirkby but not back immediately to Ops. This was because of what was known as one of the 'Moon Periods'. With the moon being at it's brightest Ops were considered too dangerous so there was a brief suspension. We were put on a series of training sorties which consisted of fighter affiliation, 'Y' bombing and NFT (Night Flying Test).

On the 16th of December we were on squadron battle orders again and the target once again was - Berlin! We were really being thrown in at the deep end as a green crew doing four operational sorties and three of them to Berlin. However, there was no complaining from the crew, for we realised that there were many other crews in the same position. For us it was another quiet trip, and after flying for eight hours we landed safely. But it wasn't a quiet trip for the bomber force, and twenty-five bombers were shot down that night including two from our squadron.

Berlin 16/17th December 1943.
There were 493 aircraft on this raid, comprised of 483 Lancasters and ten Mosquitoes. A further ten Mosquitoes dropped decoy flares south of Berlin. The bombers once again took a direct route to Berlin across Holland and northern Germany. The German controllers plotted the course of the bombers and with great accuracy. Many German fighters met the force on the coast of Holland and other fighters were guided to the bomber stream on the approach to the target. More fighters were waiting at the target area and there were a great number of combats. The bombers shook off the opposition on the return trip by flying over Denmark.

Berlin was cloud covered but the Pathfinder Skymarking was reasonably accurate and much of the bombing fell on the city. The local report says that the raid had no identifiable aiming point, but the central and eastern districts were hit badly. Little industrial damage was caused. Most of the bombing hit housing and the railways. There were 720 people killed, some being foreign workers; seventy of these were killed when the train they were in was hit by a bomb at the Halensee Station.

In the city centre the National Theatre and the building housing Germany's military and political archives were both destroyed. The damage to Berlin's railway system and rolling stock caused great transportation difficulties of supplies to the Russian Front; 1,000 wagons of war materials were held up for six days. The sustained bombing had, by now, made more than a quarter of Berlin's total living accommodation unusable.

On the return trip many bombers encountered very low cloud at their bases. The Squadrons of 1, 6 and 8 Groups were particularly affected. Twenty nine Lancasters and a Stirling from a minelaying Op crashed after their crews baled out. The group with the heaviest losses was 1 Group with thirteen aircraft lost. The squadron with the heaviest losses was 97 Squadron, and 8 Group lost seven aircraft. There were 148 aircrew killed in the crashes, thirty nine injured and six lost in the sea. Twenty five Lancasters were lost, 5.2% of the force.

A couple of days break and we were back on training with a 'Y' bombing exercise. On the 20th it was Ops and the target was Frankfurt. Prior to this Op I had a premonition that we would not be returning and I was convinced that this was it for our crew. Everything seemed to go wrong - we were briefed to take off at 16.30hrs then it was cancelled due to bad weather. We had to stand by in the mess - briefed again at 22.00hrs to take off at midnight. Everyone was fed up and cheesed off! In the event it was a very quiet trip and from then I was sure that premonitions were no good to anyone, and I took the positive attitude that we would see through our tour of operations without them. It was a relatively short trip lasting only five hours and fifty minutes and after a uneventful run we landed safely at East Kirkby.

Frankfurt 20/21st December 1943.
There were 650 aircraft on this raid - 390 Lancasters, 257 Halifaxes and three Mosquitoes. The German controllers were able to plot the force as soon as it left the English coast and were able to continue plotting all the way to Frankfurt. There were many combats on the route to the target. A diversion to Mannheim did not divert too many fighters away from the main attack until after the raid was over.

The bombing of Frankfurt did not go according to plan. The Pathfinders had prepared a Ground Mark plan on the basis of a forecast giving clear weather but they found 8/10ths cloud. The Germans lit decoy fires south east of the city and used dummy target indicators. Some bombing fell around the decoys but part of the 'creep-back' fell on Frankfurt causing more damage then Bomber Command realised at the time. There were 445 houses destroyed and 1,948 seriously damaged in Frankfurt and in the outlying townships of Sachsenhausen and Offenbach. Various industrial premises were hit by 117 bombs but no important factories are mentioned. The report stresses the large number of cultural, historical and public buildings hit, including the cathedral, the city library, the city hospital and no fewer than sixty nine schools. The Wehrmacht suffered damage to four flak positions, a clothing store, a veterinary depot and the Army School of Music. Sixty four people were killed, 111 were missing and 23,000 people were bombed out. A train standing six miles south of Frankfurt was hit by a 4,000lb bomb and thirteen people were killed. Part of the bombing fell on Mainze seventeen miles to the west and many houses along the Rhine waterfront and in the southern suburbs were hit. Fourteen people were killed. There were forty one aircraft lost, of which twenty seven were Halifaxes and fourteen Lancasters, and constituted 6. 3% of the force.

Another 'Y' training with H2S and it was Berlin once again. Again luck rode with us, and after a trip lasting seven hours and fifty minutes we returned safely on Christmas Eve, ready to celebrate. One aircraft from the squadron failed to return.

Berlin 23/24th December 1943.
There were 379 aircraft on this raid - 364 Lancasters, eight Mosquitoes and seven Halifaxes. The bomber casualties were not as heavy on this raid as they were for others, partly due to the German fighters encountering bad weather, and partly because the German controller was deceived by a diversion of Mosquitoes to Leipzig. The force of fighters appeared in the target at the end of the raid and could not catch the bomber stream. Berlin was once again cloud covered and more than half of the early Pathfinders had trouble with their H2S sets. The Markers were scattered and sparse. The Berlin report shows that only the south-eastern suburbs of Kopenick and Treptow received any serious number of bombs. There were 287 houses and mixed property destroyed. One canal cargo ship was sunk and three seriously damaged. In total 178 people were killed -157 civilians, eleven police and soldiers and ten foreign workers. Sixteen Lancasters were lost, which was 4.2% of the force.

The Battle for Berlin was now well underway and on the 29th of December we were briefed for yet another attack on the German capital. There was a long approach on this raid, a ruse devised to try to confuse the German defences. We flew within a few miles of Leipzig before diverting toward Berlin. For us it was another safe trip and after a flight of seven hours and ten minutes we returned safely back to 'Silksheen'. One aircraft from the squadron was shot down.

Berlin 29/30th December 1943.
There were 712 aircraft on this raid - 457 Lancasters, 252 Halifaxes and three Mosquitoes. A long approach route from the south passing to the south of the Ruhr and then within twenty miles of Leipzig, together with a Mosquito diversion at Dussledorf, Leipzig and Magdeberg caused the German controllers great difficulties and there

were few fighters over Berlin. Bad weather on the outward trip also kept down the number of German fighters.

Berlin was again cloud covered. The Bomber Command report claiming concentrated attacks on Skymarkers is not confirmed. The heaviest bombing was in the southern and south eastern districts but many bombs fell on the east of the city. There were 388 houses and other mixed property destroyed but no item of major interest is mentioned. Casualties included 182 people killed, and more than 600 injured and 10,000 bombed out. Out of the force, 2.8% were lost, eleven Lancasters and nine Halifaxes.

So ended the year of 1943, and 1944 arrived with no respite from air operations. After celebrating the New Year it was battle orders again and we were off once more to the Big City. Some New Year greeting for the Germans, but it was also a grim greeting for the bombers. For us it was another safe one, but for the crews of twenty eight bombers including one from our squadron it was not. We landed back at base after a trip lasting eight hours and thirty minutes.

Berlin 1/2nd January 1944.
There were 421 Lancasters on this raid. The German fighters were directed onto the bomber stream at an early stage and were particularly active between two route-markers on the way to Berlin. The German controllers were not deceived by the Mosquito feint to Hamburg but their fighters were not very effective over Berlin, only two bombers being shot down over the target.

The target area was covered in cloud once more and the accuracy of the Skymarkers soon deteriorated. The Berlin report says that there was scattered bombing, mainly in the southern parts of the city. A large number of bombs fell in the Grunewald, an extensive wooded area in the south west of Berlin. Only twenty one houses and one industrial building were destroyed, with seventy nine people being killed. A high explosive bomb hit a lock on an important canal and stopped shipping in that area for several days. Twenty-eight Lancasters were lost, 6.7% of the force.

The next night it was back to Berlin. Our luck was riding high, we had yet another safe one, but twenty six bombers including two from No 57 failed to return. We landed safely after a trip of seven hours and twenty five minutes.

Berlin 2/3rd January 1944.
There were 383 aircraft on this raid, 362 Lancasters, twelve Mosquitoes and nine Halifaxes. The German control rooms followed

the bombers all the way to Berlin which was assessed as the target forty minutes before Zero Hour. Night fighters were sent to a radio beacon between Hanover and Bremen but these fighters missed the bomber stream and did not come into action until they were directed to Berlin. Most of the bomber casualties were in the Berlin area.

This was another ineffective raid. Bombs were scattered over all parts of Berlin with the local reports stressing there were no large fires. The fire services were able to contain all fires soon after they started. In this raid eighty two houses were destroyed and thirty six people were killed. Industrial damage was insignificant. Twenty seven Lancasters were lost, which was 7.0% of the force. Ten Pathfinder aircraft were among the casualties, and 156 Squadron from Warboys lost five of it's fourteen aircraft despatched.

On the 6th of January we took a Lancaster to Waddington which was approximately twenty miles from East Kirkby and did an immediate return. On the 10th it was 'Y' bombing training again, then on the 14th it was Ops once more. We went to the brief expecting the target to be Berlin but to our surprise it was Brunswick, a new target for us. A safe trip of six hours and five minutes and we landed once more back at East Kirkby and so did the rest of the squadron.

Brunswick 14/15th January 1944.
There were 496 Lancasters and two Halifaxes on this raid. There was a running commentary by the Germans as they followed the progress of the force from a position only forty miles from the English coast and many German fighters entered the bomber stream soon after the German frontier was crossed near Bremen. The German fighters scored steadily until the Dutch coast was crossed on the return trip. Brunswick was smaller than Bomber Command's usual targets and this raid was not a success. The city report describes this as only a light raid with bombs in the south of the city which left only ten houses destroyed, with fourteen people killed. Most of the attack fell either in the countryside or in Wolfenbuttel and other small towns and villages well to the south of Brunswick. Thirty-eight Lancasters were lost, eleven of which were Pathfinders, and was 7.6% of the force.

It will be noted that sometimes there are gaps of several days or even longer in the pages of my Log Book. This was sometimes due to crews taking leave or very often bad weather which precluded flying. From the 14th of January our crew had a break of almost a month from operations, but there were plenty of training exercises to be carried out which was absolutely vital to keep our efficiency to the fore. However, on the 15th of February it was Ops once again and the target was the old faithful, Berlin. For us in our Lanc D-Dog this was a strange trip. We always had the utmost faith in our groundcrew. They had always delivered to us a serviceable aircraft. However on this trip a pre-check of equipment must have been missed out by the one of the groundcrew.

We were on the bombing run and the Bomb Aimer said the standard 'Bombs Gone!' I called him over the r/t and said the bombs hadn't gone. The reason I was so sure was that when the 4,000lb 'Cookie' left the aircraft I always felt a thump below my feet as the release mechanism operated; this time I didn't feel anything. The bomb aimer did not agree and was a little put out and thought that the bomb really had gone, and asked if I was trying to tell him his job! When we landed which was rather a bouncy affair we checked and there in the bomb bay was the 'Cookie'. The bomb aimer was still a little upset on the discovery, but he got over it. It transpired that a small section of electrical cable about four inches long had not been connected properly and caused the failure of the bomb dropping mechanism. As a result of this failure to drop the bombs over the target the Skipper and the Bomb Aimer on instructions from the wing commander had this Op deducted from their total of operations. This was a troublesome Op for us but for some it was disastrous, with forty-three bombers shot down that night, but none from our squadron. We landed safely after a trip of seven hours and twenty five minutes.

Berlin 15/16th February 1944.
There were 891 aircraft on this raid - 561 Lancasters, 314 Halifaxes and sixteen Mosquitoes. This was the first raid on Berlin for more than two weeks and was the largest force to be sent to the German capital and the largest non 1,000 bomber force sent to any target. It was also the first time more than 500 Lancasters and 300 Halifaxes were despatched. The quantity of bombs dropped was also a record - 2,642 tons.

The German controllers were able to plot the force soon after it left the English coast but the swing to the north over Denmark for the approach to the target proved too much for the German fighters. Forty-three aircraft were lost, of which twenty-six were Lancasters and seventeen Halifaxes, 4.8% of the force.

This raid was the effective end of the Battle of Berlin. Writing so far distant from the times it must be said that Bomber Command did not win this battle. Grievous physical damage had been done to Berlin and the psychological damage even greater. The German citizen knew from this series of raids, and raids on other cities, that they were at war and not immune from what other countries were suffering. But despite all the effort 'The Big City' was not wrecked from end to end as predicted by 'Butch' Harris. From the first raid in November 1943 to the last in March 1944, Bomber Command lost 533 aircraft which signalled a victory for the German defences. The morale of the bomber crews didn't suffer to any great degree but with the loss of so many crews, 'Green' crews had to be thrown straight into the battle on reaching a squadron without the usual obligatory 'Freshman' easy Op. Also the electronic aids that helped the victory in the Battle of the Ruhr were not available, and the prevailing weather over the German capital was almost always cloud and haze. When the attacks on Berlin finally came to an end Bomber Command would be employed attacking both the German mainland targets and targets in France, Belgium and Holland in preparation for D-Day. It must be said that we didn't know anything at all of this at the time, to us it was it was just another change in the offensive.

It was during this period we discovered there was a thief ranging around our quarters. When we returned from Ops we were finding that money and valuables had been stolen from our bunks. We knew it couldn't be our crew as we were always away at the same time, on Ops. Our rear gunner, Red Saigion, decided he was going to do something about it. He rigged up his service revolver with a series of bits of string and had the revolver pointed head high at the door so that the thing would go off when someone entered his room. It was a real Heath-Robinson affair. We had to persuade him not to carry out his booby trap plan as it could have possibly led to a charge of murder. Imagine if the Padre had entered the room to collect someone's belongings. Thankfully he listened to us. We discovered later that the thief was an ex-aircrew chap who had gone LMF. Those three letters were the abbreviation for Lacking Moral Fibre, in short an aircrew member who had lost his nerve and refused to fly on Ops. Going LMF was a serious charge and aircrew who had been awarded their flying badge knowing they were volunteers, also knew that they could not back out of their commitment to fly. When anyone did so the penalties were severe and degrading. After being incarcerated for some time they were stripped of their rank and given menial tasks to do, but were ordered to keep wearing their flying badge. Keeping their flying badge was a way of showing to all that he was indeed LMF. I have no comment to make about the LMF chaps, except that very very few indeed went LMF and we can all reach our limits of fear.

There was a break of four days and then it was back on Ops. We were called for a briefing and for us it was the German city of Leipzig once again. On the previous raid twenty-four bombers had been lost and it was considered to be an expensive raid for Bomber Command. This attack against Leipzig proved to be more disastrous than that on the 3rd of December. On this night seventy-six bombers were shot down making it the worst by far in terms of losses for the command. Old D-Dog was almost one of those lost. About a hundred miles from the target Frank the mid-upper gunner suddenly shouted 'Dive Skipper, fighter', just as we were attacked by a Junkers Ju 88. The cannon shells from the fighters guns ripped holes in the starboard side of our Lanc and knocked out all the electrical services for the aircraft. There was a terrific flash behind a control panel between me and the navigator and I saw him give me a black look as though it was my fault. By this time I was all hunched up in the astro dome vainly trying to reach for my parachute which was on the step alongside but now well below me. Everything seemed so quiet, just the swishing of the wings and all my past life flashing before me. I'd heard of tasting death - this was it! Yet I felt no real panic, just an acceptance! Then that lovely cockney accent came over the intercom swearing like a trooper as he and the flight engineer slowly pulled the Dog out of the dive. I remember thinking that the wings would never stand the force as we lost 10,000ft in the ensuing dive. The reason we lost so much height before gaining control was due to the full bomb load we were carrying. I clearly recall seeing the Skipper and the flight engineer hauling back on the stick with their feet on the instrument panel trying to level out the aircraft. When finally the aircraft was stable we did a check and found that all hydraulics were u/s.

We would have been fully justified in returning but the Skipper asked for a vote to see if we should abort or press on. Press on was the reply and so we did, once again I felt pride in our answer. This can also be interpreted as one member of the crew didn't want to let down the rest or be the one to say no, whichever way it showed we could do our job.

We attacked the target, dropped the bombs, and turned for home. We flew all the way back to England with a loose engine, the intercom dead and the bomb doors open as the hydraulics were u/s - although the doors opened there was no power to close them. This extra drag slowed our return and we landed back after a trip lasting seven hours and twenty five minutes. Although the losses in the command were high, only one aircraft was lost from the squadron.

Engineers from A.V.Roe, the manufacturers of the Lanc, had to repair the 'Dog' and told us that had we been airborne another five minutes the damaged engine would have fallen off. My 'Guide' was working overtime that night and I thanked Him accordingly. The Skipper was awarded an immediate DFC for this trip. Rightly so!

Leipzig 19/20th February 1944

There were 823 aircraft on this raid, of which 561 were Lancasters, 255 Halifaxes and seven Mosquitoes. This was an unhappy raid for Bomber Command. The German controllers only sent part of their force of fighters to the Kiel mine-laying diversion. When the main bomber force crossed the Dutch coast they were met by a further part of the German fighter force, plus those that had been hurriedly returned from the Kiel. The bomber stream was thus under attack all the way to the target.

There were further difficulties at the target because winds were not as forecast and many aircraft reached the Leipzig area too early and had to orbit and await the Pathfinders. Four aircraft were lost due to collision and approximately twenty were shot down by flak. Leipzig was cloud covered and the Pathfinders had used Skymarking. The raid appeared to be concentrated in it's early stages but scattered later. There are few details of the effects of the bombing. No reports are available and there were no post recce flights. Photographs taken later included the results of an American raid which took place the following day. Seventy eight aircraft were lost of which forty-four were Lancasters, thirty-four Halifaxes, 9.5% of the force. The Halifax loss rate was 13.3% of those sent, and 14.9% of the Halifaxes which reached the enemy coast after 'early returns' had turned back. The Halifax IIs and Vs were permanently withdrawn from operations to Germany after this raid.

All shades of humour abounded among bomber crews and black humour the distant relative of good old banter was very prevalent. There was one wireless/op who shared our hut who was always trying to lay on bets about who would, and who would not, come back when we were about to go on an Op. One day after the brief he came up to me and said, "Buzz, 5 to 1 says you don't come back tonight". I replied, "You're on at 10/-". I came back but I didn't get paid out as the 'Bookie' failed to return.

The sadness and horror of it all was not far away, but we laughed it away and tried to hide our real fears. On a lighter note our crew in D-Dog had a running bet with the crew of C-Charlie as to who would be FIRST back after each Op. The standard bet was 2/6 per crew member. After a few of these races to speed back home, land and taxi into dispersal, the wing commander intervened and hauled Johnny Ludford and the Skipper of C-Charlie into his office and told them in no uncertain terms that the two crews had to cut it out. We complied with the order and promptly changed the bet. From then on it was 2/6 per man for the LAST one back, the first down would report his landing thus letting the other know he was down. This in effect turned out to be a slow race where each crew would hang around as best they could (once out of the danger area) which resulted in running dangerously low on fuel. On one occasion we were very close to our limit and were just about to proceed with the landing let down, when we heard C-Charlie check in that he landed. A close run thing for just half a crown a head!

Our next Op was the night after the run to Leipzig. The bombing campaign showed no signs of relenting as Bomber Command pounded the heartland of Germany. Our target for this night was the city of Stuttgart. I gave my usual prayer on the take off run and we were airborne. On this Op I experienced a phenomenon that has never been explained and was witnessed by countless bomber crews. On the run in to the target I was positioned in my usual place in the astro dome on the look out for fighters. It was then that I saw a brilliant white flash which was especially bright as we flew right through it. We assumed we had flown through the remains of an exploding aircraft. These flashes were called 'Scarecrows' by the aircrew and were at first thought to be phosphorous explosives and were credited to the Germans who either towed them up amongst the bombers or fired them with their flak. The 'Scarecrow' was supposed to mimic an exploding aircraft. The idea being that the bomber crews would be unnerved by all the exploding aircraft around them. For me it was a most terrifying experience. After this bizarre happening we went on to the target, dropped the bombs and headed for home. I said my prayer of thanks on landing as we once again returned safely after a trip lasting six hours and fifty minutes. On inspection of our aircraft we found no debris of the exploding aircraft we had flown through. Research after the war shed no light on the 'Scarecrow' theory. The Germans denied they ever had such a thing and so it was assumed that the brilliant white flares really were exploding bombers.

Stuttgart 20/21st February 1944
There were 598 aircraft on this raid, 460 Lancasters, 126 Halifaxes and twelve Mosquitoes. The sweep round the North Sea and the Munich diversion successfully drew the German fighters up to two hours before the force flew inland. Stuttgart was cloud covered and the bombing became scattered. The local report states that considerable damage was caused in the centre of the city in the north and western suburbs of Bad Canstatt and Feuerbach. Several important cultural buildings in the centre of the city were badly damaged, the Neuss Schloss and the Landtag, the state picture gallery, the state archives, the state theatre and two old churches. In the Feuerbach suburb however, the Bosch factory which produced dynamos, injection pumps and magnetos was heavily damaged. The

human casualties were 125 people killed and 510 injured. There were nine aircraft lost, seven Lancasters and two Halifaxes.

It was after this Op that I received an order to present myself to the Station Commander, Group Captain Taffe. The order was for a preliminary interview for a commission. I duly arrived at the CO's office, and when I was marched in by the Station Warrant Officer I immediately kicked a bucket of coke near the door, which scattered the contents over the polished floor. I said, "Sorry Sir, I did not join this squadron just to kick the bucket". That broke the ice with the CO and after that the interview went rather smoothly. I left his office wondering, but didn't have too much time to dwell on the possibilities of becoming an officer as it was time to get back to Ops. We went to the brief and the tape on the blackboard showed us the target was Schweinfurt, home of the German ball bearing industry. Thirty-three aircraft were shot down that night including one from our squadron, but G-Golf, our Lanc on this Op, brought us back safely after a trip lasting seven hours and thirty five minutes.

Schweinfurt 24/25th February 1944
There were 734 aircraft on this raid, 554 Lancasters, 169 Halifaxes and eleven Mosquitoes. This was the first raid on this target which were the German ball bearing factories. The previous day 266 American B17s had attacked Schweinfurt.

Bomber Command introduced a novel tactic for this raid. The attacking force was split into two parts, with 392 aircraft and 342 aircraft separated by a two hour interval. Part of the German fighter force was drawn to the first wave. Both waves of bombers suffered from undershooting by some of the Pathfinders and by many of the Main force crews. Schweinfurt records refer to nominal damage by the RAF raid and gives a combined figure of 362 people killed for the American and RAF raids. The first wave of bombers lost twenty-two aircraft and the second wave only eleven. There were thirty-three aircraft lost, of which twenty-six were Lancasters and seven Halifaxes. A total which constituted 4.5% of the force.

I would like to relate an incident to which I cannot put a date. We were returning from an Op when the rear gunner, Red Siagion, called over the inter-com, "Where's the Green Star!?". The Green Star was a star that Red followed and watched as we were returning from several raids and we referred to that star as his company in that dark cold lonely turret. As he was in the rear of the aircraft it meant that if he saw 'his star' we were flying west - home! This particular time he couldn't see it. The Skipper exclaimed, "I can see it!" This meant we were flying eastwards toward Russia! The Skipper executed a rapid

180 degree turn and headed for home. It was fortunate that the error was spotted so soon, for if we had carried on much further we could quite easily have run out of fuel. The Skipper asked the Nav if he would take a fix using the sextant, and he was really put out when he discovered his error. To be fair to him it was discovered that the compass had become u/s after a particularly violent manoeuvre near the target. He was a first class navigator and no one held it against him.

There was no rest. The next night we were airborne once again heading to the German heartland and the city of Augsburg. The M.A.N. Diesel Works at Augsburg had been attacked once before by day in 1942 when the Lancaster had newly arrived into service. It was not a success. Out of twelve Lancasters despatched on this daylight raid, seven were shot down and several others were damaged. On that raid S/Ldr. John Nettleton won the Victoria Cross. However we were on a night Op and there were more than twelve Lancasters flying that night. Once again it was a successful trip for us and we landed safely after flying for seven hours and forty minutes.

Augsburg 25/26th February 1944
There were 594 aircraft on this raid, of which 461 were Lancasters, 123 Halifaxes and ten Mosquitoes .The bombing of Augsburg was outstandingly successful in clear weather conditions against a 'virgin' target which had only weak flak defences. The Pathfinder ground marking was accurate and more than 2,000 tons of bombs were dropped by the two waves of the force. The RAF night raid became controversial because of the effects of it's outstanding accuracy. The beautiful old centre of Augsburg was completely destroyed by high explosive and fire, with much less than the usual spread of bombing to the more modern outskirts where some industry was located. In total 2,920 buildings were destroyed and more than 5,000 were damaged, with 85,000 - 90,000 people bombed out. Among the main public and cultural buildings destroyed or seriously damaged were the old Rahtaus, sixteen churches and eleven hospitals, but all patients in the hospitals were safely evacuated. The total value of the lost works of art was estimated to be 800 million Reichmarks (£80 million). Among the buildings destroyed was the famous puppet theatre Heimebuhne Pupenschrein of Walter Oehmichen. Oehmichen recreated his puppets, and exactly four years later opened up the 'Augsburger Puppenkiste' (Packing case puppet theatre is now well known in Germany and often seen on television). There were 246 large or medium fires and 820 small ones; the temperature was so cold (minus 18 degrees Celsius) that the River Lech was frozen over and many of the fire hoses froze solid. Between 678 and 762 people died and approximately 2,500 were injured. The Germans publicised

this raid as an extreme act of 'terror bombing'. Part of the bombing of the second wave of aircraft did spread to the northern and eastern parts of Augsburg and damage was caused to an important aircraft component factory and the former paper and cotton mills which had been taken over by M.A.N. Engineering Company. The various diversions and splitting the force helped to reduce casualties. Twenty-one aircraft were lost, 3.6% of the force, sixteen Lancasters and five Halifaxes.. At least four were lost due to collision.

After five Ops in ten days we had a break for four days and then it was back to a training sortie, which was a short one hour and thirty-five minute air-to-sea firing exercise. On the 1st of March it was back to Ops with a trip to Stuttgart. For us another successful but very long sortie, and we landed back at base after eight hours and fifteen minutes in the air.

Stuttgart 1/2nd March 1944.
There were 557 aircraft on this raid, with 415 Lancasters, 129 Halifaxes and thirteen Mosquitoes. Thick cloud covered the route to and from the target and this prevented the fighters getting into the bomber stream. Cloud covered the target and the Pathfinder markers quickly disappeared into it. Returning crews were unable to judge how successful they had been, but local reports show that much damage was caused to the central, western and northern parts of Stuttgart. Several historic buildings in the centre were severely damaged including the Kronprizenpalais and the Altes Schloss. The Neuss Schloss damaged some time earlier was now completely destroyed. Much housing was hit and 125 people were killed and 510 injured. Several important industrial premises were seriously damaged including the Bosch works, the Daimler-Benz motor factory, and the remains of the main railway station hit in an earlier raid. There were four aircraft lost, three Lancasters and one Halifax, 0.7% of the force.

There followed a couple of training sorties, one fighter affiliation exercise and a 'Y' revision air-to-air firing exercise. On the 15th of March it was Stuttgart once again and like the last trip it was successful, and we landed safely after a trip lasting seven hours and thirty-five minutes.

Stuttgart 15/16th March 1944
There were 863 aircraft on this raid, 617 Lancasters, 230 Halifaxes and 16 Mosquitoes. The German fighter controllers split their forces into two parts. The bomber force flew over France almost to the Swiss border before turning to Stuttgart. This delayed the German fighters contacting the bomber stream but, when the German fighters

did arrive just before Stuttgart, the usual combats ensued. Adverse winds delayed the opening of the attack and the same winds may have been the cause of the Pathfinder marking falling back well short of the centre of Stuttgart. Most of it fell into open country south west of the city. The Akademie was damaged in the centre of Stuttgart and some housing was destroyed in the south west suburbs. Eighty-eight people were killed. Twenty-seven Lancasters and ten Halifaxes were lost on this raid, which was 4.3% of the force. Two of the Lancasters forced-landed in Switzerland.

Our next Op was to Frankfurt which was a relatively short trip of five hours and thirty minutes and a quiet one for us.

Frankfurt 18/19th March 1944
The number of aircraft which took part in this raid was 846, of which 620 Lancasters, 209 Halifaxes and seventeen Mosquitoes. The German fighter forces were again split. One part was lured by the Heligoland mining operation, but the second part waited in Germany and met the bomber stream just before the target. Low cloud made it difficult for these fighters to achieve much success. The Pathfinders marked the target accurately and this led to heavy bombing of eastern and central districts of Frankfurt. The later phases of the bombing was scattered but this was almost inevitable with such a large force and new crews were usually located to the final waves. Extensive destruction was caused to Frankfurt. The local reports give a long list of cultural buildings destroyed, including the Opera House and the preserved medieval quarters. Most of the report consists of statistics - 5,495 houses, ninety-nine industrial firms, 412 small businesses, fifty-six public buildings - all destroyed or seriously damaged; many other buildings were lightly damaged. The number of civilian casualties was 421 killed and 55,000 bombed out. A military train was hit and twenty soldiers in it were killed and eighty wounded, but this may have been the action of a Fighter Command intruder aircraft. The Frankfurt report says the train was shot up by cannon fire. Twenty-two aircraft were lost, of which twelve were Lancasters and ten Halifaxes, 2.6% of the force.

We returned to Frankfurt on the 22nd of March and like many other sorties it was a quiet one - for us. After a trip lasting five hours and thirty minutes we landed safely.

It was during this period that an occurrence involving the mid-upper gunner (MUG) the flight engineer and myself. The MUG sits on a strap type seat slung across the base of his turret, (most uncomfortable I would think). On this night the strap broke preventing the gunner from manning his turret properly. The Skipper sent the f/e to assist him. After a couple of minutes nothing was heard, so the Skipper sent me to investigate. I found the f/e slumped on the floor. He hadn't taken his portable oxygen bottle with him and so was suffering from anoxia. I went to his aid and he began to fight me he was so confused. I struggled to place my mask over his face, becoming slightly dizzy myself, but he became more violent so I did the only thing I could think of - I punched him on the jaw which laid him out. I fitted his mask onto him and went to the aid of the MUG. Somehow I managed to thread some cable through the anchor point of the seat and the strap all this while the gunner was hanging on in his turret. It seemed to work and the seat held until the end of the Op. The f/e had a painful jaw but he held no grudges and we were still friends.

Frankfurt 22/23rd March 1944.
There were 816 aircraft on this raid, 620 were Lancasters, 184 Halifaxes and twelve Mosquitoes. An indirect route was taken crossing the Dutch border north of the Zuider Zee, and then almost due south to Frankfurt. This diversion and a minelaying diversion confused the Germans for some time. Hanover was forecast as the main target. Only a few fighters managed to find the bomber stream. The marking and the bombing was accurate and Frankfurt suffered another heavy blow, the city's records show that the damage was even more severe than in the raid carried out four nights earlier. Half of the city was without gas, water, and electricity for a long period. All parts of the city were hit but the greatest weight of the attack fell on the western districts. The report mentions severe damage to the industrial areas along the main road to Mainz. The report also mentions long lists of historic and cultural buildings, churches and hospitals destroyed. Mention is also made of five important and twenty-six lesser Nazi Party buildings hit. There were 948 people killed, 346 seriously injured, and 120,000 bombed out. Sixteen B17s of the American Eighth Air Force used Frankfurt as a secondary target when they could not reach Schweinfurt some thirty-six hours after this raid and caused further damage. The Frankfurt diary reads,

The three raids of the 18th, 22nd and the 24th of March were carried out by a combined plan of the British and American air forces and their combined effect was to deal Frankfurt the worst and most fateful blow of the war. A blow which simply ended the existence of the Frankfurt which had been built up since the Middle Ages. (Source: Stadtarchin, Frankfurt).

One result of these heavy raids was that recently captured RAF aircrew had to be protected by their guards from assaults by angry civilians when they passed through Frankfurt to reach the nearby Oberursel interrogation camp.

There were a couple of days rest with a ten minute air test and a trip to RAF Spilsby and back, and then on the 26th it was Ops once again. Our target was the city of Essen in the Ruhr, the industrial heart of Germany. In the Ruhr Valley there was the notorious searchlight and flak belt which made it one of the most heavily defended areas in the mainland of Germany. We went into the bombing run and flew through an extremely strong box barrage coming from all round the city. This meant having to take pot luck and fly through the flak twice, once in and once out. The target was certainly one of the 'hot' ones. We were hit by several fragments of flak and the aircraft was peppered with small holes, some one to two inch across which was rather uncomfortable and disconcerting. But the Skipper flew on, we dropped the bombs and turned for home. We landed safely as did the rest of the squadron after a trip lasting five hours and twenty minutes.

Essen 26/27th March 1944.
There were 705 aircraft on this raid, 476 Lancasters, 207 Halifaxes and twenty two Mosquitoes. The sudden switch by Bomber Command to the Ruhr just across the German border caught the German controllers by surprise. Essen was cloud covered but the Oboe Mosquitoes marked the target well and this was a successful attack. Forty-eight industrial buildings were seriously damaged and 1,756 houses destroyed, 550 people were killed, forty nine missing and 1,569 injured. There were nine aircraft, 1.3% of the force, lost on this raid. Of these six were Lancasters and three Halifaxes.

On the 29th we carried out an air test and then on the 30th we were called for a brief for a night Op to the city of Nuremberg, or as it is called Nurnberg in it's German translation. Nuremberg had been the place for the Nazi rallies in the 1930s and so had special significance. On the way to the target and over the target we were witness to dozens of bombers going down in flames all around us. Normally we tried to keep a tally of falling aircraft with the navigator making a time fix on all the ones going down. So many were being lost this night it became impossible for us to log them all. We knew this raid was not going well and it was going to be a terrible loss for the Command, but we didn't know how bad. For us personally it was a quiet trip in so much as we weren't attacked by fighters or hit by flak and we returned safely after a trip of eight hours and five minutes. We learned later that ninety-four bombers had been shot down that night. This raid turned out to be the worst night that Bomber Command was to suffer. A further twelve aircraft crashed on the return to England, chiefly caused by battle damage on the way to the target, over the target and on the return journey. A magnificent book by Martin Middlebrook entitled The Nuremberg Raid fully chronicles the events of that fateful night. I shall never forget it!

Nuremberg 30/31st March 1944.
There were 795 aircraft on this raid, 572 Lancasters, 214 Halifaxes and nine Mosquitoes. The German controller ignored all diversions and assembled his fighters at two radio beacons astride the route to Nuremberg. The first fighters appeared just before the bombers reached the Belgian border and a fierce battle in the moonlight took place during the next four hours. The action was much reduced on the return trip as most of the German fighters were forced to land for fuel.

Most of the crews reported that they had bombed Nuremberg, but research showed that approximately 120 aircraft bombed Schweinfurt fifty miles north west of Nuremberg, two Pathfinder aircraft had dropped markers at Schweinfurt. The main raid was a failure. The city was covered by thick cloud and a fierce cross wind developed in the final approach to the target causing many Pathfinders to mark too far to the east and a ten mile 'creep back' developed north of Nuremberg. Both Pathfinders and the main force were under heavy and concentrated fighter attack throughout the raid. Little damage was caused to Nuremberg. Ninety-five aircraft were lost, sixty-four Lancasters and thirty one Halifaxes, 11.9% of the force.

On that disastrous night a Victoria Cross was awarded to Pilot Officer Cyril Barton of 578 Halifax Squadron based at Burn, Yorkshire, which was not too far from our base and in 4 Group. Barton's aircraft was attacked constantly en-route to the target and was severely damaged. However, he carried on and bombed the target. His aircraft was again attacked on the return journey and due to confusion some of the crew baled out. Cyril Barton with the remainder of his crew crossed the English coast at County Durham desperately short of fuel. He struggled to keep the crippled bomber from crashing into a row of houses at the colliery village of Ryehope. The aircraft did miss the houses but crashed into the colliery yard. P/O Barton died from his injuries and lies buried in Kingston-on-Thames cemetery in Surrey. There is a memorial plaque to Pilot Officer Barton VC in Selby Abbey.

It will be noted that after the resume of the raids from The Bomber Command War Diaries a percentage of bomber losses is given. This percentage is extremely important. If it rises above 5 - 6% on a regular basis then the losses in crews and aircraft is outstripping the replacements and which could cause a cessation in the bomber offensive. Bomber Command at this point in the offensive was running very close to that critical point. After Nuremberg the RAF stayed away from the German mainland in force for several days, but kept up the attack with smaller forces of bombers as the month of April arrived. Bomber Command licked it's wounds, regrouped and prepared for the next phase of the air battle which was the preparation for the invasion of Europe.

We carried out a 'Y' training exercise with a newly promoted Flt/Lt Ludford at the controls. John had gone straight from P/O to Flt/Lt missing out the rank of F/O. This was quite common at this period due to the losses in certain ranks. There was a change of emphasis in the bombing pattern from the beginning of April, which for us began on the 5th with an Op to Toulouse in France. The target was an aircraft factory which after the attack was almost totally destroyed. We learned later that 90% of the buildings and production plant were put out of action. On the return journey we were diverted to Boscombe Down in Hampshire and landed safely after a trip lasting seven hours and fifty minutes. This was an almost enjoyable trip flying at 5,000 feet over France with Victory 'Vs' being flashed to us by the French all the way.

Toulouse 5/6th April 1944.
There were 144 aircraft on this raid, 143 Lancasters and one Mosquito. This was a successful attack on the aircraft factory and was the beginning of pre-invasion raids at targets in France and the Low Countries. A report from Toulouse confirms that the factory was severely damaged. The marking for this raid was carried out by 617 Squadron and not the PFF. In the first low level Mosquito marking flight of the war, Wing Commander Leonard Cheshire dropped his markers on his third pass over the factory. The target was well defended but the Mosquito was so fast it was not hit. Two Lancasters of 617 dropped further Markers which were so accurate that the resultant bombing was of near perfect concentration. Most people living nearby had time to take shelter or run into fields, but twenty-two people were killed and forty five injured when about 100 houses were hit. One Lancaster exploded over the target.

On the 9th of April we were briefed for a new type of operation, that is a new type for us. The target was Danzig Bay where we were to lay mines. A minelaying Op was known as a 'Gardening' trip. They were called gardening because the mines were 'Sown' and as the mines were sown they were called 'Veg'. Our first Gardening trip was a success and I might add an easy trip although a long one. It entailed passing over neutral Sweden which was all lit up. No blackouts. The Swedes waited until we had passed over and then they threw up some flak as a token gesture. They later said we had violated their air space. We landed back at East Kirkby after nine hours in the air.

Danzig 9/10th April 1944.
There were 103 Lancasters of 1 and 5 groups on this raid. The target was the coast around Danzig, Gydnia and Pillau in the Baltic where hundreds of mines were sown. There were nine Lancasters lost on this raid.

After a few days off from Ops we were detailed for a trip to Juvisy, a railway marshalling yard and a suburb of Paris. This was another total success for us and for the group the target was devastated. We landed safely after a trip lasting five hours and ten minutes, but one aircraft from the squadron FTR.

Juvisy 18/19th April 1944.
There were 202 Lancasters, four Mosquitoes from 5 Group, and three Oboe Mosquitoes from 8 Group. The attack was completely successful. There was one Lancaster lost.

On the 20th we paid our third visit in a row to Paris. The target was La Chappelle and the results were as spectacular as the previous two. One squadron aircraft FTR and one crashed in England. We returned safely after a trip lasting four hours and fifty minutes.

La Chapelle 20/21st April 1944.
There were 269 aircraft on this raid, 247 Lancasters and twenty-two Mosquitoes. This raid on the railway marshalling yards north of Paris was the first major test of the new 5 Group Marking method, with the Group not only using 617 Squadron but three Pathfinder squadrons. A few of 8 Groups Mosquitoes were used to drop markers by Oboe to provide target location for the main force from 5 Group. The bombing force was split into two parts with an interval of one hour, with each part of the force aiming at a different part of the target. There were a few difficulties in the opening of the attack, with the Oboe Mosquitoes being a fraction late, and faulty communications. Both parts of the bombing force achieved extremely accurate results. There were six Lancasters lost on this raid.

On the 22nd of April there was a switch from targets in France to Germany. This was a deliberate policy to keep the German defences guessing and to put maximum strain on their defensive efforts. We were briefed for an attack on Brunswick and like the other Ops we returned safely after a successful trip and landed after being in the air for five hours and forty-five minutes.

Brunswick 22/23rd April 1944.
There were 265 aircraft on this raid. 248 Lancasters, and seventeen Mosquitoes. Very few German fighters were drawn to this attack. This raid is of importance in the history of Bomber Command because it was the first time that the 5 Group low-level marking method was used over a heavily defended German city. The initial marking by 617 Squadron Mosquitoes was accurate but many of the main force did not bomb because of a thin layer of cloud and faulty communications between the various bomber controllers. Many bombs dropped in the centre of the city but many H2S aimed bombs fell to the south of the city. Brunswick records that forty-four people were killed and that the damage was not extensive. Four Lancasters were lost, 1.5% of the force.

The bomber offensive was relentless. We were on operations almost every night. On the 24th of April we were on battle orders for yet another attack against the German industrial heartland and the target was the city of Munich. It was on this night we were to use another type of bomb. This was what was called the 'Oil Bomb' A specially designed bomb with explosives and oil which illuminated the area when it exploded. We were approaching the target and flying through searchlights and flak and I was positioned in the astro dome as a look out for enemy aircraft when I witnessed something that was to stay with me for the rest of my life. We were flying in echelon with five Lancasters on our starboard side about a hundred yards or so apart when the furthest one was picked out by a 'Master Blue' searchlight. A Master Blue was a radar controlled searchlight which, when it locked onto an aircraft, the free searching lights all coned the unfortunate aircraft in a mass of light. This Lancaster was immediately coned and the flak shot it out of the sky. This happened to the next four Lancs, one breaking into three sections and slowly tumbling down to earth. I didn't see any parachutes. I warned the Skipper that we would be next and he immediately pushed the stick forward and dived down and lost altitude. I am convinced that action saved us that night. We attacked the target and turned for home landing safely at East Kirkby after a trip lasting ten hours and fifty minutes, our longest trip. An unforgettable night. But our luck was being stretched to the limit. This raid was mentioned when Group Captain Leonard Cheshire was awarded the Victoria Cross. He marked the target in his Mosquito from an altitude of 750 feet. What a man!

Munich 24/25th April 1944.
There were 260 aircraft on this raid. 244 Lancasters and sixteen Mosquitoes. The marking and controlling worked well and many bombs fell into the centre of Munich. The intense flak and searchlight defences did not prevent the low level Mosquito Markers from carrying out their task and no Mosquito was seriously damaged. A German report details much property damage, mostly of public and domestic buildings rather than industrial, though much damage was done to railway installations. 1,104 buildings were completely destroyed and 1,367 were badly damaged including forty-eight public buildings, thirty schools, twenty-four police and air-raid posts, eighteen military buildings, thirteen churches and seven hospitals. Casualties were; eighty eight people were killed, 2,945 injured and 30,000 bombed out, with twenty four more people trapped in the wreckage. It is not known why the death toll was so low. There were nine Lancasters (3.5% of the force) lost on this raid.

The very next night it was Ops again. We were briefed for a raid on the city of Schweinfurt our second visit to this target. For this Op we didn't have our faithful D-Dog but another Lanc, A-Able. We did our pre-flight checks climbed on board and the Skipper taxied out to the runway. I settled in my position and the four Merlin engines thundered then we were airborne, I said my prayer asking for deliverance and we headed for the target. We went into the bombing run the bomb aimer gave the familiar cry "Bombs gone!", and we turned into the shallow dive and headed for home. As we landed I said my prayer of thanks, we then taxied into dispersal after a trip lasting nine hours. Another successful and safe operational sortie completed.

Schweinfurt 26/27th April 1944.
There were 206 Lancasters and 11 Mosquitoes of 5 Group and nine Lancasters of 1 Group on this raid. This raid was not a success. The low level marking provided for the first time by Mosquitoes of 627 Squadron was not accurate. Unexpected strong head winds delayed the Lancaster marker aircraft and the main force of the bombers. German night fighters were carrying out fierce attacks throughout the period of the raid. The bombing was not accurate and much of it fell outside Schweinfurt.

A Victoria Cross was awarded on this raid. Sgt Norman Jackson a Flight Engineer in 102 Squadron, was shot down over Schweinfurt. The Lancaster was hit by a German night fighter and a fire started in the fuel tank in the wing area. Sgt Jackson climbed out of the hatch with an extinguisher and a parachute while another crew member held the rigging lines of Jackson's chute which opened in the aircraft.

Sgt Jackson lost the extinguisher and, as both he and his parachute were being affected by the fire the men in the aircraft let the parachute go. Sgt Jackson survived with serious burns and a broken ankle. The remainder of the crew baled out later. There were twenty-one Lancasters lost on this raid, 9.3%. of the force.

That sortie was my 28th Op, but for the rest of the crew it was their 29th due to the fact that they flew on that Berlin raid earlier in our tour when I was laid up with the 'flu. When we went to have our Log Books signed a day or so later our Flight Commander signed the books and declared that our crew was now Tour-Ex. This meant that we were officially screened from air operations for some time. The normal number of operational sorties a bomber crew were expected to do before they were screened was thirty. We were screened before that number as the Squadron Commander took into consideration the two extra long sorties we carried out of ten hours and nine hours respectively, and he allowed me to be screened even though I had flown one sortie fewer than the rest of the crew. So we had survived. I was certain that my prayers had helped us through what was a most gruelling and dangerous period of the whole bombing campaign. We had flown eight times to Berlin and to the Ruhr which were amongst the most heavily defended targets in Germany. Not only that, I had flown through and survived the two most costly raids of the entire war for Bomber Command - Leipzig seventy five lost and Nuremberg ninety-five lost. I was thankful and grateful. Now my flying with the RAF was, I hoped, to be a little different and less stressful.

Crew Debrief

Chapter Four

O.T.U. Instructor.

When crews were screened from operations they were almost always posted to training units, we were no exception. However, before I was sent to a training unit I was granted a commission. From May 1944 I was known as. . . . 174575 Pilot Officer. Bosomworth. J.T.

I was extremely proud on receiving my commission. Coming from a small and insignificant village and having only a basic education, I had beaten the odds in more than one way. It was a most wonderful feeling having survived a tour of bombing operations and then being granted a commission. My early determination, conviction and faith had, I am sure, carried me through. Before being posted we were all given seven days leave, and whilst I was at home I was able to order my officers uniform at Barkers, my old firm. The uniform was to be made up by Simpsons Gentlemen's Tailors of Piccadilly, London. From there it was sent on to my station on my request. It was during this leave that the whole crew, including wives and girl-friends, were invited to a week-end party in London by the Skippers parents. So being the only married man on the crew I was able to take my new wife along to meet everyone. We were put up by the neighbours of the Ludfords for two nights and were regally entertained, going to a show and to a slap up dinner at Simpson's Hotel in the Strand - no expense was spared with taxies laid on to cross London. I discovered later that Dorothy had been unable to get leave (officially) for that week-end, but she took it and got away with it!

My luck still held... so we returned to our station and my uniform duly arrived, with the winged flying brevet on the left breast showing WAG (Wireless Operator/Air Gunner) instead of the standard winged 'S'. The WAG brevet wasn't really official but looked very impressive, and certainly different.

By mid-May 1944 I was a Wireless Operator Instructor at RAF Bruntingthorpe in Leicestershire, home of No 29 Operational Training Unit. I was what was known as a 'Shepherd', that is, in charge of a flock of twenty trainee wireless operators and charged with keeping their records up to date and looking after them, which was quite a challenge. The aircraft we used at Bruntingthorpe was the venerable Wellington, and having trained on that type I was fairly familiar with it.

The training we carried out was similar to that I did when I was at O.T.U., but with some changes as new equipment had been added. I settled down to the training role and as the summer of 1944 unfolded, with the invasion of Europe and the D-Day landings, the ensuing months were quite memorable. While I was at Bruntingthorpe a young Australian airman married a local girl and so we decided to stage a special surprise for them both. The wedding took place at Countersthorpe church, and just prior to when the happy couple came out of the church we were airborne in five Wellingtons which had to be air tested prior to night flying that night. As they stood waiting for the usual events to take place after leaving the church, we went in at low-low level on the 'bombing run' and 'bombed' them with toilet rolls. It caused quite a stir, and when I think of it and how low we flew, I still wonder why we didn't get into serious trouble. Imagine it - five Wellingtons coming in from all angles at roof top height on a 'Quiet' Saturday afternoon!

On the 18th of September 1944 I was seconded, as part of a special crew with a civilian pilot (Mr.Grierson), to fly a specially adapted Lancaster on secret trials. The Lanc belonged to a secret unit from Lutterworth where Frank Whittle (later Sir Frank Whittle) was carrying out his research into the jet engine, which of course we didn't know anything about at the time. The Lanc sported the standard four Merlin engines but quite uniquely it had a single jet engine in the tail area. For us it was something completely unheard of. When the time came to board the Lanc we were told not to look toward the tail section of the aircraft but to take up our stations as normal. This we did, and we couldn't see anything of the rear area as it was shielded by partitions. When airborne the Lanc was able to fly with just that single jet engine running while the four Merlins were shut down, yet the Lanc touched over 300 mph. It was quite an experience.

In the November I was promoted to Flying Officer but stayed instructing at 29 O.T.U. into 1945. I was then posted to RAF Wing near Leighton Buzzard and during my time there I acted as the station sports officer, a position I enjoyed as it gave me chance to play a lot of cricket. However, at the beginning of the Spring of 1945 a whole crew of instructors, including myself, volunteered to return to operations to fly as a special squadron operating Flying Fortresses. We were told that we must take our turn as there were plenty of ex-tour types who had been rested longer than us who were volunteering. Again my luck held. A crew chosen in our place were later shot down on a day-light raid and in fact the wireless operator, a newly married lad called Tommy Tate whom I had known quite well, baled out and was shot up by a German fighter pilot and killed. The Germans were becoming desperate and chivalry was gone, and so had my days of volunteering! In the event as history shows, Germany surrendered on the 8th of May 1945, and the war in Europe was finally over.

A great wave of elation and happiness swept the country at the end of the war against Germany. This euphoria was tempered by the knowledge that there was a vicious and brutal war still being waged against Japan. For those still serving in the RAF this was at the forefront of their minds, not least the bomber crews.

As it had become obvious that the war against Germany was nearing it's end, the Air Chiefs with Bomber Command together with the Air Ministry began preparing for the war against the Japanese. To this end they formed what was known as The Tiger Force. The Tiger Force was a special force created of experienced crews who had been selected and trained to fly Bomber Commands two main aircraft, the Lancaster, and the new Lincoln, for a campaign against Japan. To the relief of all concerned the dropping of the two Atom bombs in August put an end to the war in the far east and an end to The Tiger Force. The war was over and I had survived, thank God!

However, for me life in the RAF went on. I became very busy arranging and playing in cricket matches during the appropriate seasons at the Rothschild private estate in Wing village. It was an enjoyable pastime - free from flak, free from searchlights and free from stray bullets. As time went by a succession of demob parties started, as first one and then another good mate left the fold. Officers mess parties and dining in nights soon developed. Dorothy was able to come over to a couple of them after she had been given her honourable discharge when our son Richard was born in February 1945 - fourteen days over due. He would never make a navigator!

I was promoted to the rank of flight lieutenant in mid-1945 which gave me a feeling of great pride and achievement. My early determination and drive to succeed after my rejection to grammar school had really paid off, and I could face leaving the RAF with confidence and not a little pride.

I had served for close on five years and for my service in the RAF I was awarded the 1939-1945 Star, Aircrew Europe Star, Defence Medal, War Medal. It is worth mentioning the Aircrew Europe Star. This campaign medal is the only campaign medal of all the seven Stars awarded in World War Two that actually proves the holder flew in combat during the war. Every other campaign star could and was awarded to all three services, but the Aircrew Europe Star was specific. To qualify for the medal, an airman had to fly on operations for sixty days between the dates of 3rd September 1939 and 5th of June, 1944. If any aircrew did not reach the sixty days due to being shot down and made POW, or lost on operations, the Aircrew Europe Star was not awarded. Any aircrew who completed or flew their sixty days after the 5th of June 1944, were awarded the France & Germany Star. The only other medal that shows proof of air combat is the Battle of Britain clasp which is worn on the 1939-45 Star by all aircrew who flew in that memorable battle in 1940. The Aircrew Europe Star is the most rare and coveted campaign medal of World War Two.

In July 1946 I was finally demobilised and the time came for me to put the war and the RAF behind me and begin the task of finding work to support my wife and family, this was to prove more difficult than I imagined.

Chapter Five

Civvie Street

Arriving back in Northallerton after the war as a civilian was, in many ways difficult, but no more difficult than it was for any other ex-serviceman. It took time to settle down and I had to seriously look at what type of work I was going to do, in a world where there were many many others in the same situation looking for work and trying to get back to a normal life after the stresses of service life. Finding a house was extremely difficult in those early years, and so Dorothy and I had no option but to go and live with her parents at Leeming. I applied for a job with a local builder, Walter Thompson, and I was taken on as a labourer. There were two reasons for taking on this manual and very basic work. I needed employment for the money, but I also took it on to get myself back into the idea of having to graft and work physically, a sort of personal therapeutic training. I worked for Walter Thompsons for some six weeks digging ditches and all manner of holes. I was once gently warned by Walter Thompson himself that I was working too fast and if I continued to do so I might cause some industrial trouble, which I found hard to grasp. I decided that I needed something more rewarding and worthwhile. After consulting with my wife I decided to join the police force.

After applying and being accepted I was sent to the Police Training Centre at Pity Me in County Durham, arriving on the 13th of October 1946. The course was of a duration of thirteen weeks and I duly passed out as Police Constable J. T. Bosomworth, and I was posted to South Bank in Middlesborough. Dorothy and I with our son had our very first home of our own when we moved into a police house. My time at South Bank was, to put it mildly and succinctly, an 'eye opener'. I really found out how other people lived in such urban areas. Completely different to the country life that I had known in Silton and Northallerton.

From South Bank I was sent to Northallerton where I worked in the stores, and then in 1949 I was posted to Malton, that lovely North Riding market town some forty miles away. I stayed at Malton and had nine and half wonderful years. We had two more children while we lived there, Pauline who was born in 1948, and Hazel who was born in 1950. All three of our children did exceptionally well at school and passed for the Grammar School, and eventually graduated from higher education. I played quite a lot of cricket during my spell at Malton and sometimes turned out for Lord Grimthorpe's Eleven. One of the teams we once played against was a touring side of National Service cricketers. One of the many stars in this side was the future England test captain Ray Illingworth. In this particular match I managed to bowl out Ray Illingworth for a 'duck' with one of my medium pace off cutters which went through 'The Gate'. Ray managed to get his own back by bowling me out, but not before I had scored twenty five runs. Taking that wicket is one of my most cherished memories of my cricketing days.

As most people know, Malton is one of the main centres of horse racing and this meant that I was able to indulge further my hobby and interest in this sport. I met many owners, trainers, jockeys and celebrities during my nine years there, and visited all the racecourses in the area, either on or off duty, York being one of my favourites. From Malton, in 1959, I was sent to Oswaldkirk village as a country beat PC - another rewarding and memorable stay, but five years later I was on the move again.

In 1964 I did a house and beat swap with Peter Walker of Northallerton (later to become famous as the author of the TV series 'Heartbeat'). At Northallerton I became the recruiting officer and remained there until 1972 when I retired with the rank of sergeant after twenty-five years service. Whilst at Headquarters I was to try a new way of flying. There were three or four other ex-aircrew types working there, including the Chief Constable Mr. Harold Salisbury who had flown Seafires with the Fleet Air Arm during the war. A good man who was 'one of the lads' when off duty. One day he instructed four of us to report to Sutton Bank where we were initiated into the art of what he called real flying. He owned a quarter share in a glider at Sutton Bank Gliding Club. I had two quarter hour flights with the chief instructor in one of the older dual controlled models and was even given control for a short while. I found it rather eerie at first, with just the swish of the wings for company and the knowledge that there were no engines to take us round again in case of an overshoot! Nevertheless, we all thoroughly enjoyed ourselves.

I still love to fly, and like most people nowadays have done so several times on holiday. For example, Malta, Austria, Jersey and three trips to Canada, where we visited our daughter Pauline. In Canada we spent a week in a log cabin in Algonquin National Park, Ontario alongside one of the thousands of lakes. The proprietor of the site was a flying man and had his own pre-war Piper Cub aircraft on stilts and floats which he kept in a boathouse on the lakeside. I told him I was an ex-flying type and so he took me up on a three-quarter hour trip round the area. This was an entirely new experience for me, especially taking off and landing on the lake, really flying 'by the seat of your pants'. Flat out at about 75mph. Wonderful!

Then to cap it all, on my 70th birthday, instead of buying me the usual shirts, jumpers etc., the family treated me to a surprise present, and kept the secret well. On a beautiful clear Sunday morning I was transported to Teeside Airport for an hours instruction on flying in a Cessna C152 aircraft. The pilot was Mr. Edwards who at that time was the personal pilot to Sir John Hall, the Newcastle United maestro, and was also the chief flying instructor at the club. After a little instruction I was allowed to fly the thing for about half an hour and it was great! We flew over home and 'shot up' Roseberry Topping before returning to land at the airport. A most memorable birthday present.

Dorothy and I are now living in retirement in Romanby, where I follow the racing and sport in general and have the usual garden to keep under control. I am an active member of the local PROBUS Club, and with regular visits by our children and grandchildren, life for both of us is pleasant and reasonably happy.

Jack passed away 2 November 2013 aged 91.

Printed in Great Britain
by Amazon